Poems for the misunderstood and chronically underestimated woman.

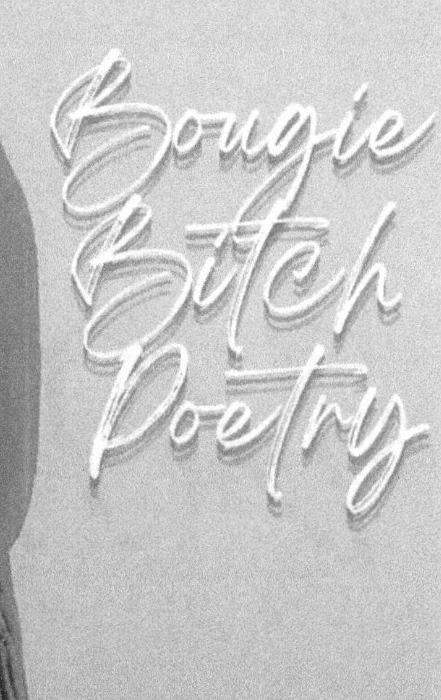

LAURA WIZE

FOREWORD BY JANUARIE YORK

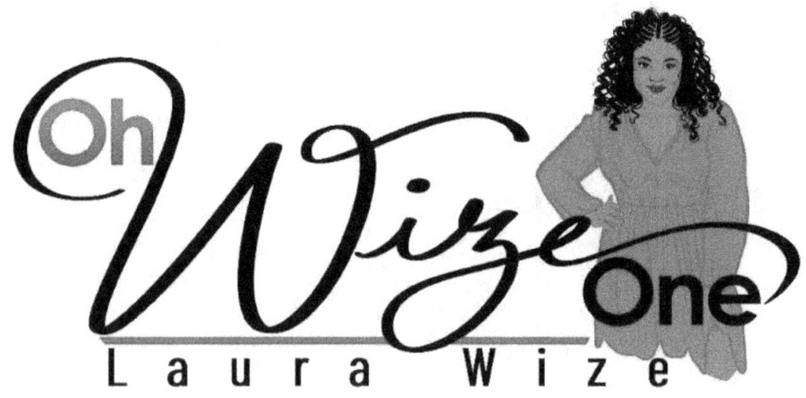
Oh
Wize
One
Laura Wize

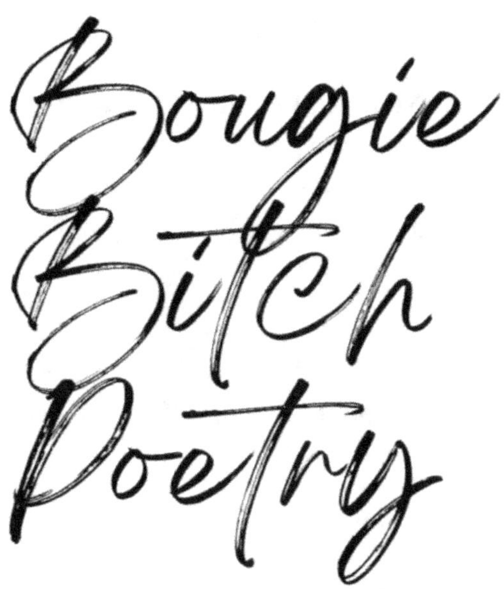

Poems for the misunderstood and chronically underestimated woman

by Laura Wize

First paperback edition September 2022

ISBN: 979-8-9851987-5-1

Foreword by Januarie York

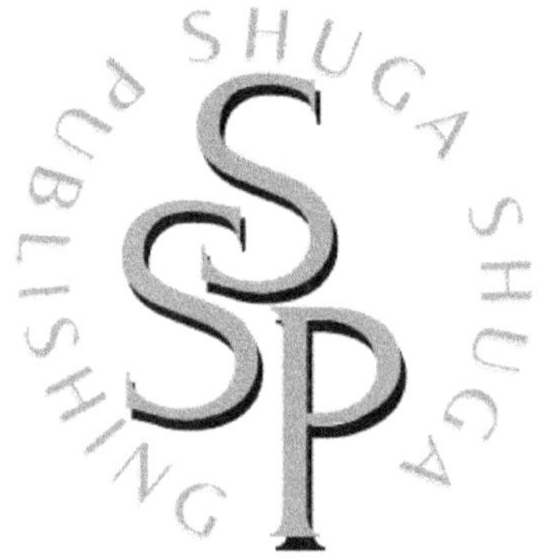

Published by Shuga Shuga Publishing LLC
ssbookpllc@gmail.com
web: shugashugallc.com
phone: (214)727-4496

Dedication

For the times I judged myself, for the times I judged others, and to atone for the times I allowed that judgment to impose on how I treat myself and others

For my mom for always loving and supporting me even when she doesn't understand

For my sister who always has my back

For my daughter for always making me want to be better

For every woman who wants what she wants

Don't let anyone make you feel like you shouldn't have EXACTLY what you want!

Table of Contents

Foreword

by Januarie York

There are levels to being a WiZe One. For most, it's just a cliché catchphrase used to describe those aging with precision. But for Laura WiZe, being a "WiZe One" is a name.

A *birthright.*

A lifestyle worth leading with the type of intention that grows flowers from brain gardens and produces eternal legacies from legendary actions. Again, I say, there are levels to being a WiZe One. For sake of keeping things classy, cute, and with just enough Bougieness to open this book properly, I refer us to Merriam Webster's definition of the word "wise."

Those **levels** I referred to are outlined in perfect text here: *"marked by deep understanding (1), keen discernment (2), and the capacity for sound judgment (3)."*

Through her wonderful and international world, Laura WiZe exemplifies each tier of her last name in its adjective form. She glides into the room as if her feet were individual magical rugs, braided coils sweeping the side of her face, and brandishing a dimpled smile that could make the hardest scowl turn bashful blush. Stages fall to her mercy, allowing her voice to rebuild the floors they once stood on. She understands the vision of her life and isn't afraid to play with its (re)creation as necessary. That ability to discern and make good judgement calls allows her to leap into the air, reaching for the highest resting fruit she can grab.

For an artist of any type, this is key to being limitless.

Laura is the inside of a poem; the space between the first and last stanzas, where the lines run together, each letter holding hands, and creating a church choir worth of sound from the created lyrics. Her voice carries in three-part harmony; a poetic meltiness that prepares the listener's ears, a playful sauciness that pours out like perfected aged Bourbon cascading over sphere ice, with just enough bougie to inspire a lifted pinky to join a Hollywood sip of imported, chilled champagne. If you have ever seen a live painting at a poetry show, Laura is the living version of the painting, and she's inviting all of us into that painting.

Welcome to the legendary house of Oh WiZe One.

This is the runway show bitches!!! Selections are presented in the order of which they need to be received. Black women and girls are represented through a transparent, regal lens with each chapter afforded its own showstopping entries. It's a marriage of Black girl inner-culture (our culture within our Black culture) to the fullness of our life experiences.

The poems that follow will walk the page runways wearing couture content and dressed in descriptive colors and lyrics that flow like iridescent pearl chiffon fabric. The collection is only as seasonal as the emotions that connect with it – the range in this project will activate the spirit of the "carefree Black girl" in all of us.

As *wise* as the levels she was predisposed to, Laura has intricately woven the poetic melodies of her heart's songs to present a harmonious garden of Black hope, feminine and oh so divine! As you open to receive the wisdom between these pages, sit up a bit, stick your chest out, and let your shoulders back.

Give your head a side tilt and a slight smirk just before extending your hand to grab a crumpet. Keep a crumpet nearby – Bougie Bitches love crumpets!!!

I'd even suggest throwing on a cute high-low dress with some vintage tea gloves.

You're not just reading a book of poetry; you are headed into an experience, where the peaks and valleys will be compliments of icy blue skies that hold cloud pools for the sun to take a rest behind. *I know.* That was an unnecessarily extra sentence.

Bougie Bitches love being extra.

You are now entering a continuous climbing altitude. An area where discernment, understanding, and sound judgment are the set precedence to this peace offering. As you venture through, my prayer is that the love of sisterhood, relatability, and the wisest takeaways are as much in abundance for you as they were for me.

It's not just a safe space; it's a WiZe one, and there are levels to this shit.

Preface

Words of the WiZe

Why does labeling something or someone give the human brain so much satisfaction? A human behavioral expert would go into great detail and explain survival instincts. They would tell you all about how you inherited these instincts from your ancestors and blah, blah, blah.

If life has taught me anything, it's shown me that we love to label things because we want to know what something is and how we should treat it. You put ketchup on fries, you hang coats in the closet, and you put Black women in their place. You read Bougie Bitch Poetry on the cover of this book, and you had a reaction. GOOD that's exactly what I wanted.

Black women are quick to be labeled ghetto, angry, strong, or difficult, and if you dare like nice things, you're bougie.

I've been called a lot in my lifetime but bougie is always rising to the surface of casual observations of me. It could be the restaurant I recommend for lunch, the way I dress, or the way I set my expectations. If there is any inclination that I want something other than what people feel I should have, it's bougie.

I scrolled the internet for images of bougie black girls and images of well-dressed Black women filled the search engine. Black women eating brunch, sitting at picnics, drinking wine, working, and shopping. I was overcome with rage because these women weren't doing anything excessively fancy.

What's bougie about eating pancakes?

Who knows what hell that well-dressed black woman at brunch is dealing with? Is she nice, empathetic, charismatic? No one cares because she doesn't appear to be struggling, so she must be fine. Who does she think she is sitting there existing without visible pain?

Labels like that make you dislike someone because once you've categorized a woman, you know what you can do with her. You can "not like" her and after a prolonged period of not liking a woman at some point you'll start to wonder, "who does this bitch think she is?"

My poetry in this book is answering that question.

Who does this bitch think she is? I am a product of my environment. I am the living projection of the desires of my heart. I am a lover. I am an ally. I am an enemy. Most of all, I'm just like you and something about that bothers some people. I'm just a bougie bitch trying to live my life.

Can I live?

Dear Black Woman,

I have created this space to allow you to both survive and thrive as your most bougie self.

What if we changed the narrative for a bad bitch?

Allowed her to range from Angela Davis to Angie Stone, to Angela Rye, and Angie down the street.

I do the most because even when I hold back, it's a lot

I've barely spoken but I've said too much

On one hand, advised to accept nothing less than what I want and on the other hand, I'm told the price is too high

Told my taste is too expensive so I should scale back my requirements

Told I should be more realistic

Told I set my sights too high and I'm out of touch

What made you think I was approachable?

I've been called frivolous because of my appearance

Did you get a scholar when you wanted a bimbo?

Is it because I have a fancy for fancy things?

Does the way that I carry myself make you assume that I think I'm better than you?

Was I born into the wrong class or pedigree to have an affinity for these things that seem so commonplace to me?

Am I fancy or did I just make an effort?

What's so bougie about me? Is it the boundaries I set?

Is it the way I dress or the food I eat?

Please tell me about myself. Label me in a way that makes you feel more comfortable about your future mistreatment of me - Take me a little less serious

Is this disinterest in the "real me" your coping mechanism or a way to conceal your admiration?

Do you like nice things or do you like what you think nice things say about you?

Because in here we let the money talk and bullshit walk

I'm just here to spread 'pay her bills' propaganda

Bandz will make me dance but paying my bills will make me chill

Adding value to my life is always right

I stopped letting these people think loving me doesn't come with a cost - That's a scam

I'm just bold enough to seek freedom beyond perception

What seems like cockiness is just ointment for my visible vulnerability

I'm heartbroken more often than I break hearts but labeled hard to love

Pulling price tags off new dresses as the uncertainty of my life hangs in the balance

You don't know me well enough to know

That I hate systematic special treatment that only awards a few

Because special treatment is counterproductive; it breeds fake love and real hate. We all deserve a treat

I am more concerned with quality experiences than awarding only an elite few

A wise woman said, What I want for myself I want for my sista...And what I want for my sista is what she wants for herself ... as long it ain't hurting nobody

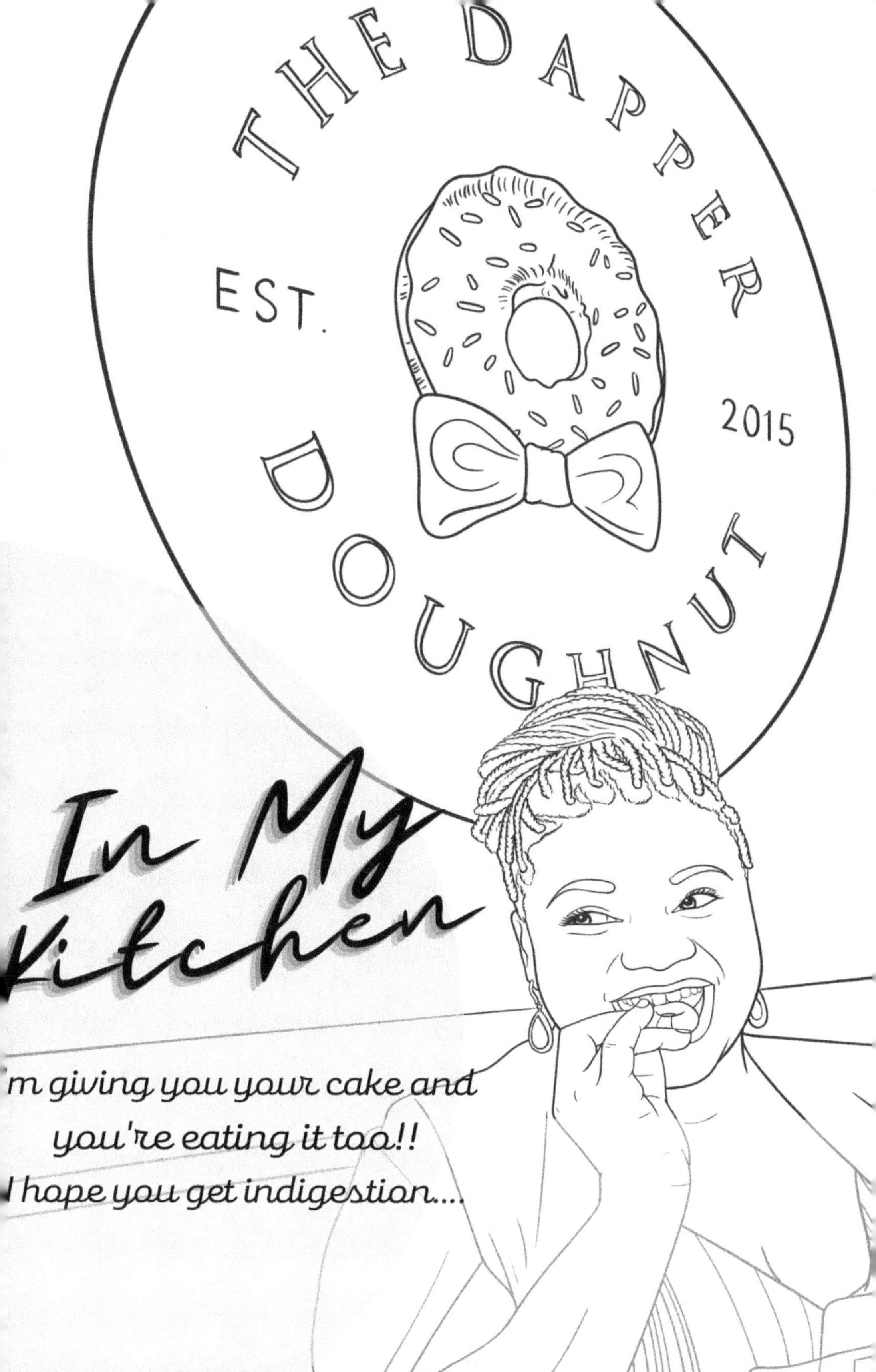
THE DAPPER
EST.
2015
DOUGHNUT
In My
Kitchen
m giving you your cake and
you're eating it too!!
I hope you get indigestion....

Spoiled

So immune that you don't
realize

Once removed from your
system you'll be an apple's
core, exposed and rotten

Who will salvage you then?

My sweetness erodes your
essence leaving its mark
behind

It's going to be hard to
substitute me

Once the well runs dry, and
the cake is consumed,
you're full

Devour another piece
Who else will let you feast?

I'll just watch you eat and
clean your plate

Don't let any of me go to
waste

Overdose on my sucrose

Fiend for the way I make you
feel like you got wings

So accessible,
always available,
no honey,
no molasses

Just me

Almost too sweet to be

I wonder what happens when
it all ceases?

You without my sweetness

Throw a tantrum

You can't have me before
dinner - you have to monitor
your intake

It won't be the same with a
duplicate. A copy of a copy
never comes out as sweet

Plus, all the others claim they
taste just like me

Maybe you'll grow bitter in my
absence

Sour over your saltiness

This sweetness has ruined you

I spoiled you

Candy Coated Confessions

Remembering

It's the only way we can stay close,
grabbing memories like kids clutching
candies

Removing wrappers of reality
discovering bittersweet pains

Powdered sugar-covered confections
and midnight confessions leave our
wet skin sticky with residue – this
makes me remember

You can have my last lemon drop in
exchange for a tear; an emotion to
cover the burning sensation

The awful aftertaste
pungent purgatory
distinguishing then from now

Public defense mechanisms
transform into private surrenders
wondering who will give in next
with arms outstretched

Ready to let each other regress

Admittedly depressed

Despite how well dressed the
treats are, sugar-sweet tones
quickly grow cold

Our affinity for reminiscing
overcomes our ability to dismiss
each other

You're addicted to my voice box
I'm addicted to your spirit

Love's candy necklace left behind
multicolored evidence that makes
it evident

Closure can only come when you
want something to be over and my
dear - the candy shop is still open

The Real Reason Ain't Nobody Got a Man

Cookies in abundance
I got 2 for 1
10 for 5
What you lookin' fo?
What you want?
What you need?
I been cookin' in the kitchen
I got that fresh out the oven
Postin' pics of home-cooked meals,
Cookie
I got that work

I got that all night
Do you right
Soft and chewy, moist on the inside,
individually wrapped
I got that free sample, walk
around the store, come back to my
kiosk I'll give you another Cookie

Wishing
Hoping
Planning
Praying
Preying

Cookie - I got it

That accepting, selfless, unconditional
love
Cookies fresh out the oven
I got a whole sheet

Fresh - Waiting on you to take a bite
I got that all night

Got that "let's build a community with
all your baby mamas"

Suck your dick in public, right in the
comment section

Support your small business that really
ain't a business; got that full-time job,
Cookie
Let you follow your dreams

That sit on the couch, play X-Box, eat
up all my food, Cookie
That let you cheat long as I don't
see, Cookie

That you mean more than me,
chocolate chip, honey dip, butterscotch,
even though you be gone you can come
back home, Cookie.

I'll make tacos Jody

That butter pecan, let you keep that
side dip, Cookie

I just can't see you without me, Cookie

I can't breathe, Cookie
I can't sleep, Cookie
I can't eat, Cookie
Without you in my life, Cookie

I been waiting all this time, Cookie
I can't even focus on any other aspect
of life, Cookie

I ain't got no stamps in my passport,
no sense of self, can't find the root of
the problem, Cookie
whispers It's me

That he ain't brought my car back,
late to pick me up from work in my own
shit, Cookie.

I can't figure out why no one will pay
retail for this cookie, Cookie - even
though I've been giving it away for
free, Cookie
Got that fuck these other bitches
They ain't on my level
you should eat my cookie, Cookie

I'll hold you down - ride or die, Cookie

Self-righteous, saving it for Jesus,
giving it away in the dark for potential
marriage proposals, Cookie

Surplus Cookie
Cookies in abundance
The market value's low on cookies
The stock has plummeted, Cookie

We're all out here in a single file line
waiting to give our submission to the
next nigga passing by because it beats
being alone, Cookie

Who stole the last Cookie from the
cookie jar?

Learn to Cook

Young, unmarried with a child, my mother and aunts filled me with
scripture and urged me, "learn to cook".
Said, "It's better to marry than to burn.
Ain't no man gon marry a woman who can't cook."

So, at 18 I subscribed to Family Circle and Woman's Day magazine,
not Cosmopolitan. No matter how I increased my skill, my articles
went unread...my domestic domicile resided in the wrong jurisdiction
because 20-year-old men don't care what you cook like.

So certain that my Suzie Homemaker abilities would help me
replace the father my baby didn't have, I strengthened my game.

At 21, graduated from soul food and got gourmet.
Flipped my cheap pots and pans and hustled up Williams-Sonoma
cookware.

Properly set the table for a formal occasion and made fresh floral
arrangements so when brothers bought me dying roses from the
flower man at the club, I was less than impressed.

Seasoned myself with more than spice
Sweet to the taste and pretty in the face

Cultured conversations that span the typical
"How was your day baby?"

My oven was preheated - I was at the right temperature to cook
anyone's freak. Paired well with wine, both expensive and high
grade; the cheese stood alone at family functions.

Sunday, in the back pew taunted by the young well-dressed couple. The mother's butter-cup complexion, the father's dark hue, and their milky baby cooing, "na na nah boo boo." Set my heart to flame.

At 22, I could flambé, but one seat
at my dinner table remained vacant.

The design I was structured after is outdated or in the wrong venue. Clinging to religious views to catch a man felt like cheating God. Besides, all the cute brothers at church were married, plus I didn't exhibit the purity required.

Worldly suitors lacked the need to build a life; just passing ships in the night. The walls of my kitchen were restricting me to something I could not be.

Still unmarried; these cooking classes ain't accredited. Can't put them on my resume. My homely characteristics seemed like a repellent.

Constantly told, "Wait for companionship. Reserve your expertise". I studied hard for matrimony and feel overqualified and underemployed.

Dated more excuses than solutions.
More questions than answers.
More sickness than remedies.

Patience is my missing virtue, but it does not deter me from being available for my missing link.

The question is not can I cook, but King, are you worthy of serving?

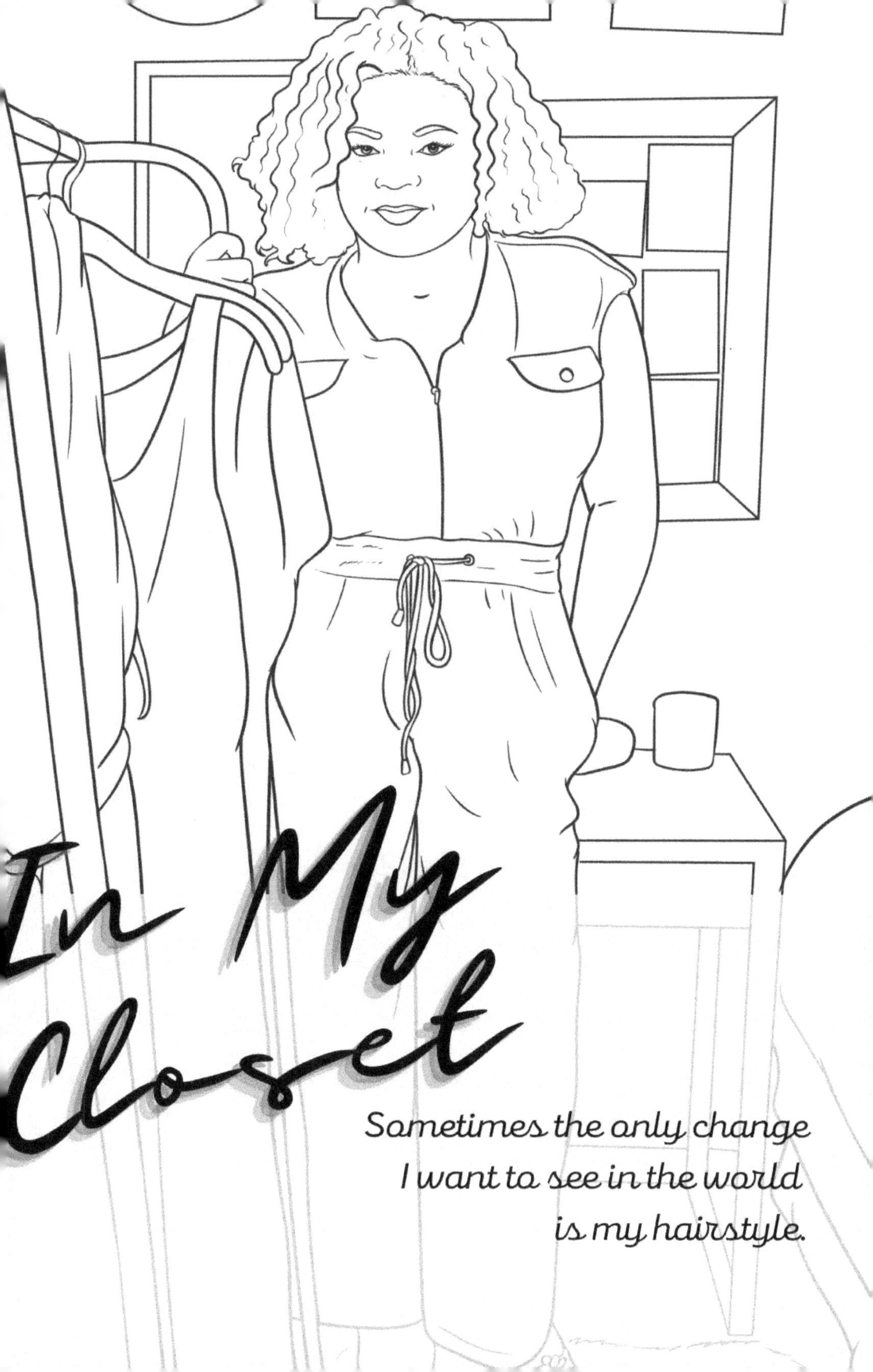
In My
Closet
Sometimes the only change
I want to see in the world
is my hairstyle.

Cardigan

Don't mistake proper attire for lack
of sexual desire

Never underestimate a woman in a
cardigan. Tricks up my sleeve will
have you begging, "do it again."

Unzip my shift dress, I will show
you the rest

Just because I'm not overly exposed
doesn't mean there's not a hoe
under these clothes

Don't applaud me until you've been
turned out -Until you tap out

Don't hold back. You can pound me
until the point of exhaustion

Spit to reignite me

Blaze me for round two; we're still
not through

Tell me nasty things you want to
do, it's not an intrusion

The freak you see is not an illusion
Spank me and see if it's real
Thinking I didn't have enough
points to handle your scorecard?

I exceed expectations, fog up
glasses, make believers out of
doubters, turn shy guys into
screamers, and cause so much
damage you'll have to call FEMA

I've got a dirty mind, a big ego, and
follow-through

Classy clothes and fishnet
pantyhose

Princess seams, whips, and chains
I take dick like payroll taxes
Give you CPR after you drown in
my ocean, second your emotions
Smooth skin from scented lotion
Tongue kisses and whipped cream
in the kitchen

Didn't think you'd get all this
from a girl dressed like a
librarian?

I'm not stepping over a threshold
not properly clothed. You shouldn't
see me naked before the end of
the night. Maybe you should learn
how to undress a lady

Never underestimate a woman in
a cardigan

Pull the string and destroy my
sweater

It only gets wetter and better

Brick House Dreams

I tried to talk to my boss about getting a cost-of-living raise

To which he replied, "Raises are based on merit."
I'm trying to get to the bag - Run up a check
Because girls can't pull fine-ass niggas just because they got clout

No amount of money can pull the man of your choice - Men see with their eyes and touch with their hands. They rely on visual lust
I need to get the money so I can buy a body

Cash is king

I need an ass that will stretch Lycra to its limits like stacks of cash stretch rubber bands
My personality ain't bringing em in the door

I'm not worried about the maintenance
I always had that on deck
Men can't see my winning personality in my jeans

Pretty faces come a dime a dozen
I carry myself like a top dollar bitch but, men don't care how I dress. Men want to know what it's hittin' for

Men care about waist to ass ratio; I ain't got it
I need a fat ass for advertising purposes
I wonder if that's tax-deductible
They say, "It's what's on the inside that counts", but if your body doesn't have any curb appeal, it's gonna be hard to get a man to come to your open house

Damn these white girls gettin' thick
Checking prices on Brazilian butt lifts
Risking my long-term health for a short-term turnaround -
Working two and three jobs

Stacking my dough

I want an ass so fat you can see it from the front
Maybe then he can get close enough to see I'm really a nice girl

I just want to begin, but I ain't got the ends
Every time I see a girl with nice dimensions, I feel the rise in inflation

Who cares about what books I've read? Who cares how well I can cook when you can get a bad bitch with assets that appreciate? Let me get to the gym and do some squats so I can plot on the finest man in the room

I see how they move - I know what they do

I just want to attract my ideal customer
I'm such a solid investment but clearly, I need to diversify my portfolio; the cost of living is going up
and, I can't afford to be passed up by the guy of my dreams

It's not about what you are made of, it's how you're built

As it stands, I can't get a man because of the way I am structured so every night I talk to God

"Now I lay me down to sleep, I pray the Lord my soul to keep and when I wake, please answer these brick house dreams."

Silk Press

It's October 9th, 87 degrees, but feels like 95.
Too much humidity in the air to straighten my hair
I just want it to feel like fall

It's been 10 summers and 9 winters
Yet, his face is all I remember
He's so wrong

Wrong like summer weather in late fall
No matter how seasons change, things remain the same
Hot when it should be cold - Cold when it should be hot

Wrong like a car wash token
when you were searching for a quarter;
he's a currency I can't spend

Heat I can't enjoy

I just want to change my hairstyle
because variety is the spice of life
That's why he could never choose me

Every tear cried over our lost love
must be trapped in the air
making it a waste of time
to pull out the heat protection

Fried, dyed, and laid to the side
I've got thoughts my flat iron can't straighten out

Hot ass vapors surrounding me making me feel like surrendering

What's the point of styling when we'll just recoil in the same pattern of this love/hate predicament?
Reverting to our original, unrequited state where I was always the giver

This weather's so unpredictable. I don't think a protective style can save me
Stressful residual emotions from this unexpected commotion - A predisposition to this deep condition your presence has always caused

Talking when I wanted you to be quiet,
picking and choosing

You're the hair that's out of place,
coming close and then refusing to be what I need
No matter how well we gel you still fly away
even when the month suggests a season change

Saying you love me sounds like summer in winter
Lies instead of the truth

I just want to change into a woman
who never loved you this deeply
Experience seasons
where my heart won't wither from needing you

You're imprinted on me
It won't change
The sun's shining
I see cumulus clouds in my peripheral
Looks like the devil's beating his wife
Rain will only make this heat stick

I've been trying to clarify us every wash day
Yet, there are traces of you on my strands

If it could only cool down enough to straighten my hair.
Never thought this bad hair day would last
Praying for an overcast so I can press my hair silky
straight, slick down my edges, flip my bangs in the direction
of another nigga looking my way, and forget about this
unseasonably warm weather

Fabric of My Life

My mother is the descendant of washerwomen
That is not a metaphor. There is a trail of washing
water that puddles from Mississippi to Alabama.
Women who washed garments and prayed to be
healed from the hem of his garment - my mother is
their reflection

Filled with their fear
Filled with her own
Filled with their wisdom
Filled with her own

She laundered her clothes to keep them looking new

Her eye trained to find quality in piles of discards
My mom hates wrinkles - She steams cotton like she
wants it to pay for the pain it caused her ancestors
My mother is the descendant of washerwomen
Keeps stacks of Vogue, Harper's Bazaar, and
Women's Wear Daily. The way she can match fabric,
sew seams, adjust hemlines - Must be the revenge
of her bloodline who were Denied entrance into
stores that sold firsthand silk charmeuse and
duchess satin

My mother is her ancestors' wildest dreams
The way she presses seams nice, flat, and beautiful

Washerwomen who may have never forced a
grommet through denim for Levi Straus; their
circumstances may not have given them the
foresight to see past ironing the shirts of rich
white men

The starch of oppression kept food on the table and
that was enough to be grateful, but my mom
envisioned fashion

My mom woke up early on Saturdays to watch
haute couture and study the lines of the
seamstresses who didn't walk the runway but made
the style possible

My mother, the descendant of washerwomen
taught me how to distinguish between a Simplicity
or Butterick pattern

My mom taught me the algebra of fashion because
too much piecework multiplied by expensive fabric
and divided by her free time meant no new dress if
the pattern was too ambitious

My mother, the descendant of washerwomen gave
me the education that her lineage taught her

My mother, she is the fabric of my life

In Need

Desperate single woman in need of a relaxer and a fill-in
Days rise and nights disappear
Trying to remember the fall
Appears we lost it

Desperate single woman in need of a relaxer and a fill-in
She tallies the bills, picks up extra work,
and attempts to have standards in a free market

Desperate single woman in need of a relaxer and a fill-in
A little less shiny than other girls
She wonders why she has to do it by herself
She might accept relationships a little less than mint
A shade lighter than "meant to be together"

Desperate single woman in need of a relaxer and a fill-in
Tax time splurges come once a year
On the brink of cashing in her chips when it's 'go hard or go home'

Life gets real
Friends with benefits ain't all that beneficial
She'll juggle the bills and settle before the ruling
Time waits for no woman, so she'll settle for that fill-in
Men chasing her with professions of love seem like a fantasy - 'Alone' is the new reality

The last of a dying breed will be buried with her morals and high standards. Her counterparts will attend her burial funeral fresh with pressed tresses and a full set

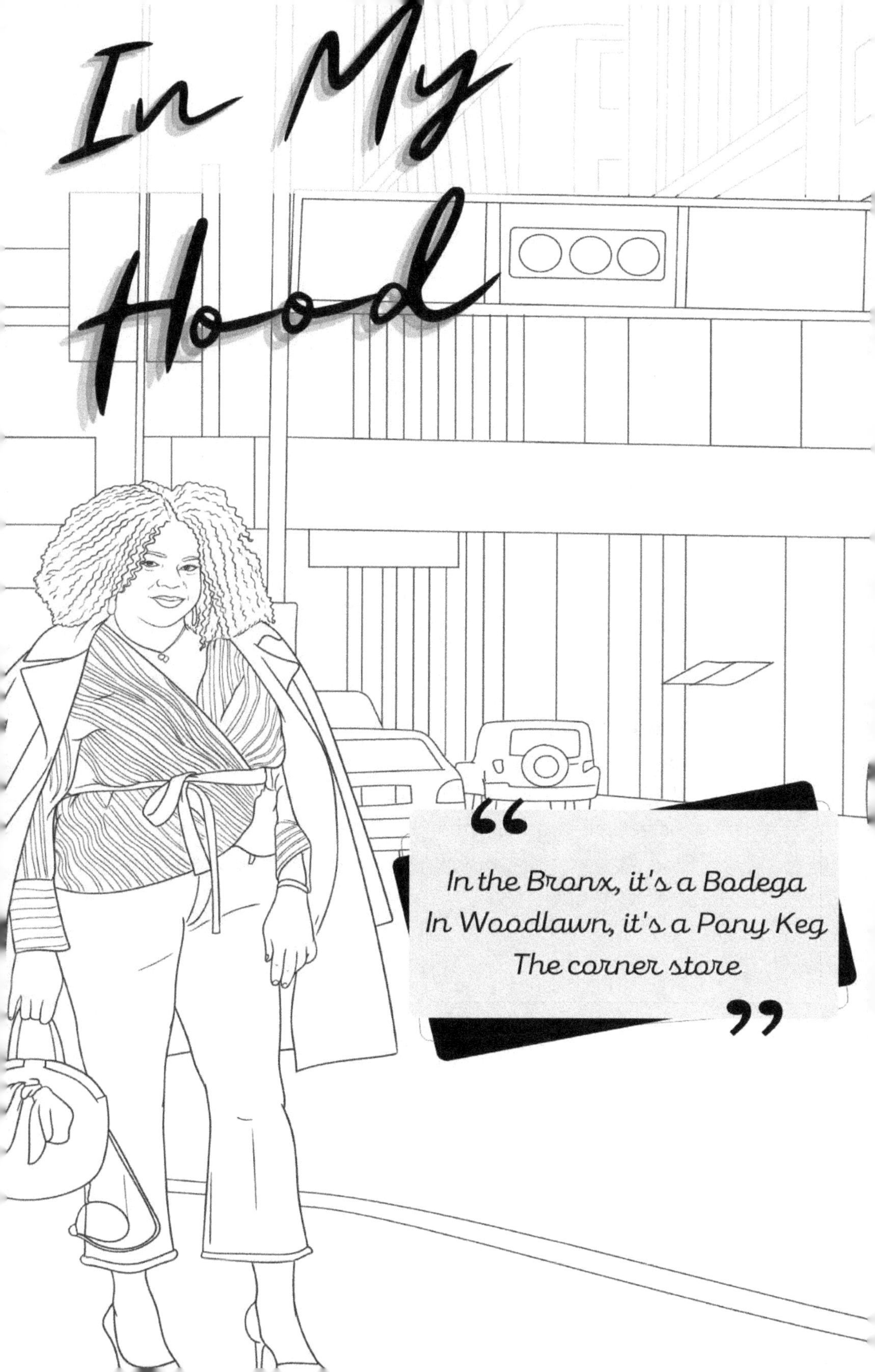
In My Hood
"In the Bronx, it's a Bodega
In Woodlawn, it's a Pony Keg
The corner store"

Best of Both Worlds

I stole my swag from church wives; From women who said things like, "never let them see you sweat"

I grew up around Black couples and Black love
Around men who took pride in how well they treated their woman. Granted some of that was rooted in misogyny but at the time it sounded good to me

Have you ever fallen asleep to the ambient noises of a church sermon?

A two-parent household didn't seem like a rarity when the wages of sin are death. Did you ever get into trouble for treating offering call like a fashion show? You would have thought the center aisle was a runway

Church wives treated decorating their homes like a competitive sport. It always kept my mother on edge, but she has the kind of class you can't buy. When other women were claiming they had the best husband in the church, my dad was at work making sure we had the best he could afford

My poor parents just wanted to be in the ranks of the well-respected saints, but their child was a rebel

A questioner of the pulpit
An asker of
Why can't we do this?
Why can't we do that?
Troublemaker
A shit starter
I never found a biblical text that supported red lips meant desiring a kiss. This all could have seemed like a passing phase if I had come out right, but life has a way of leading you down a path that affirms people's confirmed bias

I thought I was ready for the world, but I was sheltered

A rebellious church girl is still tame in a lion's cage
A misfit amongst miscreants
A harlot amongst the holy
A truth no one is ready for

I suppose I have the best of both worlds

Hey Pocahontas

I spent my morning laying hands on a purpose
At daybreak, we gathered in the garden at the heart of the hood

We all heard its heartbeat
Warm concrete and wet soil
I noticed her before she even made her way to us
Her voice loud - Filled with obscenities
I smiled, got back to my duties
Nodding my head to the dope boy's music

She crossed the street to help our busy hands
Removing weeds, planting flowers, pruning bushes, making beauty amid an abandoned block
She's beautiful but unaware of it
I was tempted to tell her, but instead, I simply welcomed her
Her hands with ours, she fell into the mix
Her hair; beautiful

She had a molly in her right tit, and a dime bag in the left
She spoke with the reverend smiling and said, "God knows my heart."
Given the liveliness in her walk at this hour of the morning, she hadn't been asleep

She was a living poem and didn't even know

One of the volunteers mumbled, "That's why you never do drugs"

I wanted to scold his tongue but educating him would have scared her beauty so, I held my peace

Four cat daddies on the corner called out for her, "Hey Pocahontas!" She shifted, swayed, and moved their way

I found a new purpose in her garden
Discovered why flowers envy weeds
Flowers need tending to and are limited by their species
Along comes the weeds, stubborn, ugly, and rapidly growing
Growing and towering over the flower; frustrated by its beauty and inability to outgrow the weed, unaware that weeds aren't welcome in gardens
They usually have short life spans
Someone will uproot them at some point
Then again, some weeds don't get plucked up from gardens as they should

They choke the flowers, causing them to die prematurely
A flower may live wishing it was a fast-growing weed that rapidly climbs up buildings where everyone can see

I saw a weed and a flower manifesting in one woman
I knew her real name wasn't Pocahontas
So, when four cat daddies called her, and she came to their call, I didn't judge her because we're all just one situation away from experiencing the next man's struggle

Hey Pocahontas, you left before I could tell you

You're beautiful

The Carefree Black Girl Section

Can someone please direct me to the carefree black girl section?

Oh, there isn't one? Well, that's not hard to believe because I don't know a Black woman without a side hustle. I don't know a Black woman that hasn't been afraid; don't know one without an open wound who hasn't been told to "keep it moving" like she ain't been sliced by life.

I laugh at the thought of a carefree black girl running through the meadow with natural hair flowing in the wind
She'll be running freely, picking wildflowers when she sees blood-soaked leaves; her lover hung from a tree - We know the deal

In exchange for love, she might suffer a slap in the face, a disgrace to her ego, and shame on her name. Nothing cuts the unbreakable bond of racial unity like misogyny.

I am here to free my sisters, understanding that many don't know they're slaves; slaves that eat misogyny for breakfast. Male-dominated lies are stuck in their digestive tracts; they're constipated.

Can't eject that shit from their system. You can't call your sister a hoe but claim you want sexual freedom. I wish you would break these chains, but you won't. Why? Because you want a man to call your own.

The way the Black male life span is set up, you might not get one. When you live in fear, you get loved in fear, never getting what you want - settling for what's here. She could find liberation in the sacrifices, but she's scared. Scared and won't go to church.

Scared and won't pick up a self-help book, won't wake up for Super Soul Sunday, or stay single long enough to hear herself. Won't take a second look at her reflection, and respect it for what it is.

I wish I could gather my sisters and march them to freedom with a gun on my shoulder. Gather all the single Black females addicted to retail, trying to fill the void with designer labels and property deeds.

I wish I could gather those sisters trying to fit the mold just to get held at night, the sisters left with post-traumatic stress syndrome after accepting bullshit off brothers who never deserved them in the first place

When nights get cold while racing north to freedom, barefoot, with no shelter; when she can't see the forest for the trees, when it feels like she might never get married, and she turns to run back to myths, lies, and propaganda; I'll point a shotgun in her face reminding her she can't go back. Her only option is death.

If she never finds self-worth she might as well be dead. If she isn't content with the rhythm of her own life, she will never dance to the beat of her own drum. She won't find a love that won't hurt her if she doesn't love herself first.

Even if a companion isn't on the other side of this underground railroad, there is love, because she is love.
You are loved. If by no one else, you're loved by me

Sincerely, Your Sister

P.S Come meet me in the back. I found The Carefree Black Girl Section

Diego On My Mind

I often stare at your faces on the silver screen. I gaze at my phone, scroll through pictures, and scream with giddiness over how fine you are.

I wonder if it's the light or the angle making you look this good. I try to get back on track, pick up my pocketbook and walk down the hall.

I step on the elevator, and you walk in looking and smelling good to me. You get off one floor before I do. You're gone but I revel in the glory of seeing you. I move on.

I'm driving home and I see you walking or
slowly riding your bike across the street.
You gained a little weight but you're still cute.

Saw you doing pull-ups at the crosswalk.
Stared a little too long at the gym and
accidentally made eye contact. I thought to myself, "Let me look the other way".

Peeped you talking shit with your friends in front of the corner store. Y'all were laughing and smoking Black & Milds.
Rolled my windows down to smell the smoke. You're nostalgic to me, like cream soda Fagos and sacks of penny candy.

You're as fresh as a pair of brand-new Jordans fresh out of the box with tissue paper and all.

I saw you on the news. You looked familiar to me. In the county jail visitation room, you all look like somebody I know. You're familiar to me.

Black men, I'm so attracted to you
no matter where no matter when. Whenever I see you, I'm pulled in like I have no choice. It's involuntary that I choose you before I can gather a thought.

Like God hypnotized me to want you. Like it was by design. Damn boy, you're fine. You are a beautiful man. Your Uncle is fine as hell too.

You're painted on my forehead. All your names must be Diego. I love you deeply. Love you strong. But loving you hurts like Sade's tattoo. Feels like you're always gone. Gone by a gun. Gone by choice. Gone by circumstance.

Every time I see you, you look like a part of me. It's funny because you don't even recognize me.

Did you forget that I was your ally?

Luck Be a Lady

If luck be a lady, she will smell of a
whore in the witching hour after
turning her last trick. Walks with a
switch on Lucite soles. Fur coat and
bare ass in below zero weather.

Bent over, back arched for your
delight. Runs her tongue over her
teeth to check for semen, white
smile beaming, price tag dangling
between her legs. She be expensive.

She will let you buy her on the low,
but you got to be ready to go. If
she be a gamble, you be a roll of the
dice at the whim of her mercy.
Pliable. She be flexible, moving in the
direction of consumption.

She be bluffing. She's huffing
between your legs trying to
exchange momentary paradise for
currency. Currently, she's got a two
for one special, she'll do you and your
friend too, just bring him with you.

She brings her own Vaseline so you can stick her even when she's not aroused. She's guaranteed. No money down, no credit check, liability-free. If you're not happy... well that's not an option. You'll get what you came for and leave with more than you came with.

It's raw, it's hurting, but keep going. It's the point of no return. Let her loose ends lull you in. She can pretend, she can be real, you can tell her what you feel. She'll keep your secrets. She will hit you, beat you until your words pull the safety.

She'll let you contaminate. Discharge all your fluids. Keep it translucent. She's fluent. Your request is on the menu. She will serve you more than you could ever get at home.

If luck be a lady, she'll be yours for the night, but only for the right price.

If luck be a lady...

Approach Me

Approach me like an OG
Approach me like a Don

Approach me like we took our first
steps out of slavery together

Approach me like Betty and
Coretta never remarried

Like for 31 years, Merlie fought for
Medgar until justice reigned
Approach me like I'm your mirror
reflection - Like I'm flesh of your
flesh, bone of your bones

Approach me like you was birthed
through my canal son, disrespecting
me is disrespecting yourself

This blind ride or die status left me
with a victim complex

My unconditional love has been
raped. My vulnerability molested.
You only scream my name when it
suits you

I watched them beat you.
It hurt my spirit to see you
dehumanized

I tried to understand when you
limited my humanity

This position has left me voiceless
and bitter - Trying so hard not to
be angry but my wingspan is weak
from circling this runway with no
place to land.

Brother, won't you catch me?
At least approach me better?

You glorify my body but scandalize
my name. You've made morality and
respectability a prerequisite
While upholding no values of your
own

Expecting to charge all your
indiscretions as growing pains

Charge your unfaithfulness to the
game - One bad mark on my part
and I can never be saved

I'm offered no grace and you never
held a punch. My ego has been
bruised. My virtue has taken a
brutal beating

My patience has been fertilized and
I am starting to grow past you
I swear I only wanted to love you,
to uplift you, to build with you
Reach higher heights
Be your wife

Inside every misguided sista using
her body as a meal ticket is a
woman trying to mold herself into
what you said you wanted.

She heard your 'call and response' on
the radio

She's trying to back it up for you,
but it's stunting her growth

She's trying to bust it wide open
for a real nigga, but you closed the
door on her

More than anything else in this
world I am yours

Approach me

Approach me like I jumped brooms
with you when they wouldn't legally
acknowledge our love

Approach me like I reached out for
you as the auctioneer said "sold"

Approach me like I held our son's
dead body as his killer walked free

Approach me with the utmost
respect and dignity because more
than anything else in this world

I am yours

Things End Badly

Do you know why Fran Drescher is so pleasant to watch on The Nanny? Nothing about her or that show emotionally decimates you. That show will never break your heart, never make your chest ache, and there's no unyielding agony from watching the unthinkable.

It's constantly pleasant. It's refreshingly predictable; unlike real life. Real-life is agony. Real-life is like a true friend, it stabs you in the front. You see it coming but the pain still seems worse than you could have anticipated.

You think you're ready but you're not.

Season one will seem uneventful. Season two will give you hope. Season three will make you regret being foolish enough to hope.

It will prove that the previous seasons were sunny days before a hurricane destroyed everything.

Real-life is a documentary. A 'based on a true story' movie meant to reveal an ugly truth; some stories don't have happy endings. Like a Spike Lee movie that ends before a definitive conclusion.

Maybe the point was there is no end because nothing is ever over. Bad shit happens every day.

The addict never recovers.

The abandoned child never gets a family. The man seeking redemption never seems to achieve it. The hero dies.

The more life you live, you grow desensitized to things ending badly, leaving you unable to empathize because... It be like that.

A man killed his girlfriend and carried her out of her apartment in a body bag down a stairwell like a sack of dirty laundry. You will see a nation in peril. Babies die. You might even turn on the news and find out your boyfriend is dead.

If you need me, I'll be catching these cheap laughs, watching unrealistic happy endings, and finding comfort in predictable plots.

So, forgive me if I can't watch an Oscar-worthy performance of a story that doesn't end well.

I can't watch tragedy for sport as easily as I used to.

I'm at a crossroad. It seems like "good things" are what happen to other people. I'm feeling like sunny days are the predecessor to a torrential downpour of hurt.

I'm tired of bad news. Exhausted from being a Black woman completely stretched out, and I'm uncertain if I have the elasticity to bounce back from being inundated with unpleasant realities.

Occasionally, I take a break between the showers to laugh at a girl who's got style, who's got flair, who's there.

A flashy girl from Flushing,

The Nanny

Questions

I wonder if a piece of a shattered
masterpiece is still a masterpiece.

I wonder if fragments of dissertations
are still literature.

Is a second of a song a sample?

Is a poem just an interlude? Is it just the
precursor to a scene? Does it not stand
alone?

Half of a statue, is it still an Oscar?

Is acclaim praise if it's not critical?

If these words never get me paid
are they worth anything?

Was the climax the crescendo? Or have I
not reached my height?

Will I get to the top by walking my own
path?

If my poem is not about what you want
to hear is not good?

Value, is there any?

Is the peace noble without the prize?

Do you only like my words when someone else speaks them? Or is it just the way it seems? Do you not want to hear them from me?

Is my genius destined to be behind the scenes?

I'm not even center stage in my own art. All spot and no light. A cute break between the music. Sounds good when it's mellow, but no one wants to slow down their thinking to listen.

Where am I?

Where are you?

Can I get your ear?

Can I address your fear?

Can I get in the rotation?

If they play me, will you change the station?

Why do I need a cosign; an endorsement from a corporation overproducing and manufacturing plastic, "made in China" versions of the classics?

I'm giving unadulterated. Do you want a simulated man-made woman instead?

I got soul. Do you want a pretty face instead?

I got depth. Do you want easy to read instead?

I'm thinking about burning these notebooks or keeping these words for private confessions. I'm feeling like devoting my time to a more profitable venture.

Is this piece of a shattered masterpiece still worth anything?

What's super glue worth if you have no intention of piecing anything back together?

Is a painting worth anything if it's not hung on a wall? Is it still art?

Behold the unseen beauty of a female poet. Pay her no mind. She's just another broken masterpiece.

Queen City

if you can't roll with a queen
then kneel at the sight of the thrown
when entering her south entrance
...her crown is the skyline
whether it's dimmed by fog
or shining brighter than the sun

The underground railroad's north star
The great migration's platform
The root so badly forgotten
that they can't appreciate the limbs
can't swing from her vine
she is too fickle to let you enjoy the ride
predictable she ain't

can't make up her mind
her seasons change every five minutes
one hundred and ten degrees in the shade
degrees of separation are below zero

this is the city where the dividing line
between Welfare and wealth is a train track

You can hate her for her limitations
or adore the gemstones buried in her character

it's a hundred thousand men
doubting her by appearance alone
her stature is deceiving

she is pretty-faced, naïve,
and from the outskirts of the kingdom
With one foot planted in the zone
the other on the globe
the key to this city only turns
when it is in optimism's hand
believe in where you stand

her fifth avenue ain't
painted by designer boutiques
she can't tell 'ready to wear' from couture
she's just excited her bag has a name on it
she's easy breezy
and two dollars on a Tuesday

so many murmurs about where I live
I love every crevasse
the city feeds me well

she keeps the light on for me
when I enter the south entrance
When you cross the Brent Spence kneel
You are in the presence of royalty

long live the Queen City

In My Heart

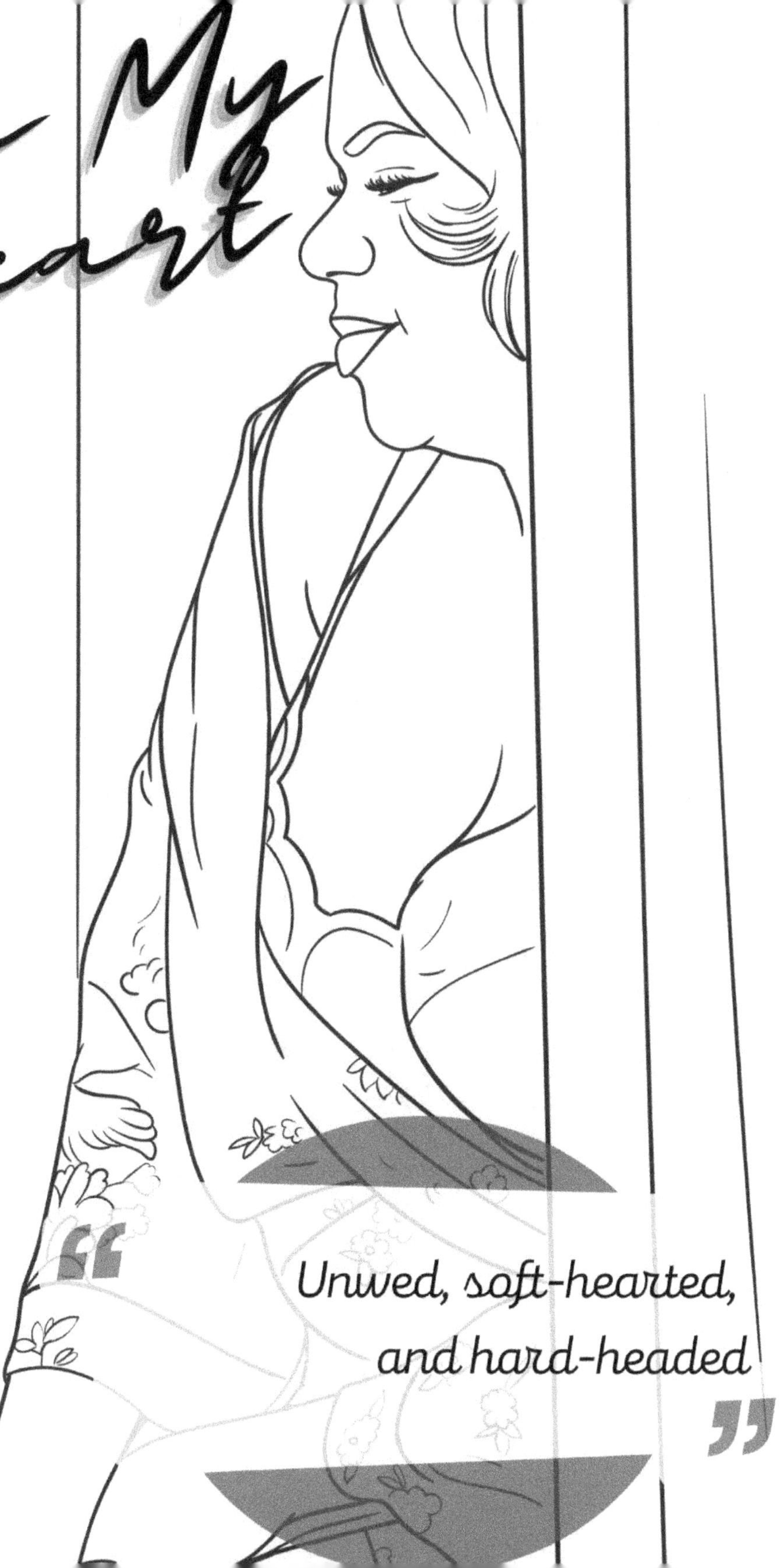

"Unwed, soft-hearted,
and hard-headed"

Act Write

When love cut my spirit, it was easy to bleed on the page. Making the lines cry was effortless. In-house dick acting right and I ain't got no sad poems to write.

Love,

I think I'm scared to sing your praises for fear that the song may send you away. Afraid you might get caught in my melody's current and float away with my rhythm. What would I dance to without our beat? Who would I cook for if you didn't eat? Why would I cut us short if my pen was always the knife? I'm trying not to use words to check our vitals.

So, I grow quiet. Tumbleweeds pass through my dry pages; my pen likes sad songs better. Playing Phyllis, Amy, and Billie just don't feel the same.

Love,

Please understand that I love what we have. The covenant between us is often unwritten, feels like it's not for my pen to document. Contentment has momentarily silenced me. In-house dick acting right and I ain't got no sad poem to write. They say poets require unrequited love; I craved oneness. You nurtured me with reciprocity, my cup runneth over.

I don't have a sad poem in me

Love,

I may have some sad poem residue. Before the sad poems were love poems, words of urgency and desperation pleading for love to bring more love only for it to run in the opposite direction with all my affection. I'm sure my pen isn't the jinx.

My ink lacks celebration. My withdrawal is a reflex that has outstretched itself into the form of writers' block. My in-house dick is acting right, and I ain't got a sad poem to write. There is an abundance of faith in our union.

No more pleading for what I don't have. So, until my pen empathizes with a subject worth writing about, I'll remain quietly in love.

Calls in the Night

Said I wouldn't call. I did.

I hear all the words in the back of your
throat never released from your lips.

Say you don't love me? I say you a lie.

We avoid each other
When you come close, I feel you wanting
my voice
I deny you because I know you do
Besides all my friends were standing there
I'm only strong cause they won't let me be
weak

Sorry I didn't speak
They were all judging me
I can't live for love
So, I'll live for expectations
This humiliation isn't that bad
You can come back

If being with you is a dream
without you is a nightmare
I know they might stare
I don't care
Pathetic

Said you couldn't see a day without me
You must be blind by now
You never have answers when I ask how
Baby, you can come back now

I won't let them put us down
My pride says it's unfortunate
that I still let you wear the crown

The Sun

I have been worried about saying this
I've learned from my past
I know the effects of giving birth
prematurely

I can feel your warmth from 93
million miles away
I can be satisfied with your smile for
days

I can tell a lot from your ways
I'm deeply affected by our exchange

I have the protection of knowledge
itself

I don't want to be burned by your
rays

I keep running to climates where you
stay

Wearing a big hat and shades, trying
to impress you with my sashay
You keep shedding light on
subjects, broadening my view

Creating deeper avenues for me to
see
I am trying not to stare at you

The sight of you leaves stars in
my eyes

Your heat leaves sweat between
my thighs
Too many seasons without you,
and tears fall from my eyes

This temperature is too hot for soul
food

95 degrees 100 percent humidity
serving me collards, macaroni, and
cheese, with yams

your nutrition is sticking to me
I'm growing

I couldn't have predicted it being hot
in the middle of winter

Ain't never met anyone who would
give me August in December

Trying to downplay green grass,
flowers in my garden, and tan lines

All out of season

I'm tripping trying to figure out
the reason

I'm sprung like spring

Mercury breaking the barometer

Sugar on the floor, and it's melting
fast

Hoping that this handshake heat
will last

I hear the clock tick-tocking

I'm not sure if it's explosive or if
it's just time elapsing

Every time we meet, I gasp from
the heat, never thirsting for water

Going faster than a bullet from a
gun - 93 million miles away

Boy you brought the sun

You keep bringing my earth justice

Existence

I want to meet a nigga who's gonna let me talk my shit
Not just let me talk it, but gleefully anticipate it
He would need to be a Teflon Don because I talk more shit than a little bit
I hope his heart keeps a tight grip
My whit would keep a smile on his face
My whip appeal would make his heart skip a beat

He'd rather caress my mind than my ass
He would still want me to back that ass up
He would adore how I ain't too bougie to get hood, and I ain't too hood to get bougie
He's highly impressed at how elegant my pimpin is
My 'fly' don't intimidate him cause he tryna match mine
He'd stay stacked up
It would never be tricking because he would always have it
Quick to put money in my hand
A new purse on my shoulder
Support my dreams
Calm my fears
He'd rep me like I'm his favorite team
He'd take a knee for me

If anyone told him to boycott me, he'd
faithfully watch over me

Loyalty

Any time I'm ready to dip, he'll provide the
sauce
He'll let me know when I've taken things too
far without bruising my ego
Takes pride in knowing his woman
Flex his knowledge like wealth
He's probably a reformed gangsta or
transformed preacher cause me and a square
nigga never stood a chance

It may feel like forever, but he'll show up
right on time - Black Thomas Crown Affair
Crash a million-dollar boat just to watch it
splash
If I don't like the weather, he'll change it
If I don't dig the environment, it's time to
go
If I'm uncomfortable, he'll address
it because transparency is necessary

Staring at me from across the room, ready to
whisper something in my ear, unlocking
what's only for him

Know when to give me my space and when to be up in my face
Low cut Caesar with deep waves
Speaks with a southern drawl or East coast slang - Most importantly, he'll speak my love language
Ready to love me in high definition
I've always been a good woman
It's time that a man showed up to be exceptional and raise the bar

To show me how them other niggas was lames
Cause I ain't said nothing slick to a can of oil
Game recognize game
What's understood don't need to be explained
A real G wouldn't need me to be tame to know that I'm the love of his life
Truly I need acceptance as I am
Cause I can only be me

I need an OG who knows the game
Who's excited to call my name
In the meantime - I'm just waiting on the universe to align me with my favorite nigga

Penny Loves Kenny

Penny is 14 years old, and tomorrow she'll be a whore

Nobody ever told her it's the wrong way
Don't worry about her, with the quickness, she'll get laid and her panties will be frayed cause it's the wrong way

Penny loves Kenny
It was love at first sight
Staring at him from across the street
The way the sunlight shined around his face
even God was making him look good

She chased him around the hood
Until he understood her intentions
To be his and eventually a Mrs.
Kenny dismisses her advances

Kenny is seventeen years old
He has no time for childlike fancy
But it was something about Penny
Something pure that he can't put his finger on
So, he lingers on

Penny loves Kenny
To keep Kenny off the older girls
she lets his man-child expectation
become her downfall

Penny lies to Kenny all the time
Told Kenny she wasn't a virgin
Told Kenny she's 15 instead of 14
Disregarded her upbringing for Kenny's up
keeping

Keeping Kenny felt like freedom

Felt like oxygen when you're drowning
Penny lets Kenny sex her crazy on the daily
Eventually, she's pregnant with Kenny's baby

Kenny said it can't be his
Kenny said he can't have kids
He discarded Penny like Penny disregarded her
virginity

That's the thing about statutory rape
It doesn't mean the girl said "No"
It means the man was old enough to know
better

Penny's 16 years old, and tomorrow, she'll be a
mom. Everybody knows that she did it the wrong
way

All Penny knows is the love on TV and the love
she sees at home

No one ever warned her that love can be
led astray - Penny comes home to a crib
and an empty bed.

The winter on her windowpane sends chills
up her spine, and she thinks that's where
a man should be, but all she sees is boys
rejecting her for bringing life into the
world

Nobody wants to play stepdaddy while
she's forced to be a mom

She confuses her self-doubt for self-
worth
And is convinced she is second class to all
the other girls

Penny dates down
Penny gets hit around
Penny invests time in men like stock
Waiting on her return but karma burned
Penny

Penny dies inside when she sees
daddies with sons walking by

Wondering how long she'll have to pay for
her sins, Penny goes and gets born again
Praying it will wash away every bad day
but the baptism only took the sins
not the circumstances

Penny hasn't seen Kenny in eight years
Penny is scared all her fears will manifest
throughout her whole life

Penny searches for the man who helped her in
conceiving believing that if she takes his life that
she'll get hers back

Penny has the right to conceal and carry
Hoping that the steel will steal back
every lost artifact of who she used to be

Penny's twenty-four
And tomorrow she'll be convicted
Nobody ever told her it was the wrong way
Don't worry about her
She released a thousand doves
on the day he was laid to rest
Cause it's the wrong way

She gave him all she had to give
but he still wouldn't take it
Salty tears run down her makeup
as the gavel rings
We the jury find Penny
GUILTY

.........of loving Kenny

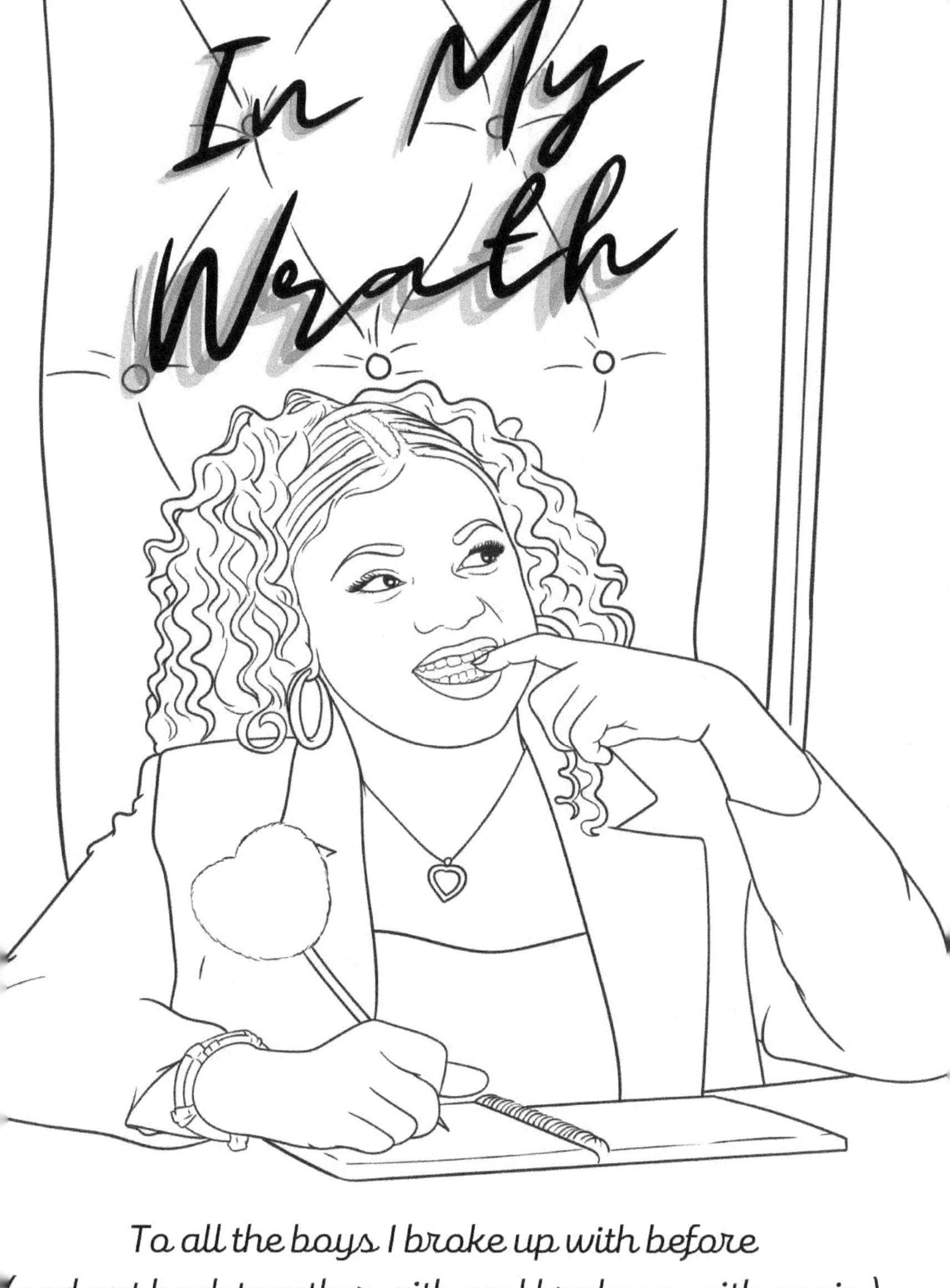

To all the boys I broke up with before
(and got back together with and broke up with again)

Nympho

At some point, I realized it's easier for us to fuck
this out than talk it out
All the times your mouth didn't have an answer,
your dick did
Put my mouth on you
Now that's a two-headed monster
Voices inspire sin
Let my ass, tits, and grin be your consolation
Where's my consummation?
If you are what you eat
how does it feel to be me?
We could turn the tables, but if it's right it
wouldn't be tight
I'll accept the wrong
My sex drive has a fast vehicle
so, where to?
Your place or mine?
I don't have time
Right here is fine
Don't be scary. You know you like my vulgarity
Your erection is proving me right
Listen, I don't wanna fight or talk about the
other bitches you like
All the women you encounter are assorted colors
and flavors
I should remove myself from the pack
I'm tired of competing with the other lifesavers
You claim I'm the one you savor
Boy, Bye

I just need you to scratch my itch tonight
I got an affliction
You got your clothes on
One of us needs to lose some of our inhibitions
Perverse visions fill my mind
Like a drool line from your tip to the bottom of my lip
Possessed by your demons
Moans transform into screams
Because as wet as my pussy is,
I can't please you
No trick can stop you from tricking off
I don't have enough voice to go off
So, my caress is me crying out for help
Your stroke is an apology
We're communicating
I don't know how to talk to anyone else like this
I mean, no one else fucks me like this
Stick out your tongue and give me a kiss
You're never missed
You take advantage of the fact that every time you enter and exit, I can't process
I'm about to come
You're about to leave
Everything and nihility
Multiples of zero; we add up to nothing
Everybody has their something
And we're busy trying to figure out whatever that is
Until then...we just fucking

Side Effects of a Colonized Heart

All those nights lying next to you. I rested
well and felt so safe unaware that I was
sleeping on the jungle floor. Somedays I feel
misunderstood. I used to think that you got
me. You know? Like really got me.
I thought I found acceptance.

I think about that night in your bed, I
couldn't keep my eyes open, like a child fighting
sleep. "Can I have a glass of water?", I
begged, trying to stay up a little longer.
Stay up and talk to you but I was exhausted.
Closing my eyes to you smiling at me. Every
time I opened my eyes, you'd kiss my lips
softly. You kissed me to sleep. I can see how I
mistook these connections as intimacy.

I still feel the weight of your comforter warm
on my body, sweet to my soul like a lullaby filled
with down feathers; all those nights sleeping
in the wild. I'd lay down with you tonight, but
I can't afford to be on safari when I know
the dangers of encountering a colonizer.

I be missing the friend that I had in you
I be needing that understanding
That kiss when I opened my eyes felt like
reassurance

That smile as I closed my eyes,
felt like recognition.
Like somebody saw the real me and liked it.
The unpopular parts of me felt they found a
home in you. I felt discovered.

Even though I was already there, you
Columbus-ed me. I thought you had an atlas to
my heart the way you colonized my
expectations of what it should feel like.
Somewhere along the way you jumped off
course. Our time set sail.

I can't get caught sleeping on the Jungle
Floor; I'd be in danger. Uncertain if I should
call the police or a priest. All these nights of
mean sleep leave me restless.

It's hard being a girl, especially when I can
only be me. It was almost suspicious; you knew
me too well. You took the time to understand
me. Colonizers learn the lay of the land to
manipulate the landscape ensuring the
elements work in their favor.

I was the sleeping prey.
You lured me into captivity.

You made sleeping on the jungle floor feel like
love in a king-size bed. This explains why I
can't get the thought of your nighttime kisses
and false acceptance out of my head.

Love Injury

If love were an injury, I'd need a handicap sticker, a walking stick, peroxide, and ace bandages. I'd need more than my Primary Care Physician. I'd need a specialist.
I'd need a neurologist to see what's wrong with my brain.
A dermatologist to check my ass from all the smacks I took trying to be a good girl for "daddy."

If love were an injury, I'd be too nervous to play the field. Thoughts of taking a hit from a player twice my size, afraid of jumping too high fearing crash landings.

If love were an injury, I'd need high blood pressure pills, high cholesterol pills, painkillers, and vitamin D.

If love were an injury, I'd need a cast on my heart, tissue for my nose and eyes, a sling for my arm, and an inhaler for all the times love took my breath away.

If love were an injury, I'd need an antibiotic for all the ghosts I tried to hide that turned around and haunted my body. I'd need a detox. I'd need a deep cleanse, and an enema for putting up with all its shit.

If love were an injury, I'd deserve worker's compensation, reparations, disability, social security, a structured annuity, and accidental dismemberment.

Can somebody call the authorities? Like damn, can't you see that love is hurting me? Love is a criminal who remains at large.

Injury, although painful, will heal. It's my responsibility to see when I'm getting in my way; I'm tripping over my own shoelaces.

If love were an injury, I'd need time for recuperation, rehabilitation, and new revelations.

If love were an injury, during the healing process, I'd watch the playbacks and be able to see when I balled too hard and took on more than my body could bear. I'd know not to push myself so hard. I'd train to have more strength so that one day I could play again.

If love were an injury, I'd return highly anticipated, glorious, a star player, heavyweight champion of the world.

If love were an injury, I'd be the comeback kid because in the end, a player's gonna play. It's all about recognizing when you have a worthy opponent.

Restraining Orders

Lovers like us need restraining orders.

Not even hate can make you seem unappealing. It only sparks the charge of intensity. You can't be in my space. I can't be in yours. We can't be alone. One word would lead to another.

I've always struggled with the ability to say no to you and mean it. The last time I said no, your face was inches from mine. My mouth said "no", and my breathing pattern said "yes". You said, "Baby, you gotta stop doing that." I knew right then that you had me. I melted like ice cream in the sun needing to be licked, dripping down the cone, running along your forearm. Handle that and get me before I'm gone because lovers like us need restraining orders.

We need time, space, and distance. We need Iyanla Vansant, counselors, a therapist, and suspecting family watching what time we go and what time we return.

Lovers like us need restraining orders.

It felt like you were only inside me for a moment, we had sex like one continuous motion. I can never recall how I went from the front to the back, how I went from being laid out in ecstasy reflecting on what you just did to me, to being drug down the sheets by my thighs.

We never ate food in bed. You were so damn tasty. The sight of you unbuckling your belt brought me to my knees, always prepared to worship at your temple. It was cultish, pseudo-religious.
I think I'm going to hell for some of that shit.

Your sweat was chocolate sauce dripping down all over me. Your breath in my ear was the cherry on top sending me over the edge.

Lovers like us need restraining orders.

I love players and you love the game. You like to manipulate, and I'm pliable like clay. I often think to myself, "I don't know if I can live without this type of passion in my life." It was so good that I lost my mind. Every good record has a B-side and the reality is, I lost my mind.

Lovers like us need restraining orders

Grammatical Errors

i love u in a way that you should never
love another human being i just wanted
to punctuate what we made, put a
period. where u placed a question mark?
crooked and confused oftentimes i felt
used but it was u

i tried constantly to improve so i could be
something u couldn't lose, indispensable
and separate from the others outlined in
"quotation marks", and accented with
exclamation! our contemporary
brainstorm was supposed to be
temporary but your implicature
proceeded, your suspicions aroused,
questions were posed, responses remained
the same, my heart exists in vain

i screamed, "i'm leaving you" (Untrue -
the comments should have been
surrounded by parenthesis leaving, is an
unproven hypothesis....) i can't escape

despite the lie in the center of your
belief, despite my positive prefix, you
provided the negative suffix, so we ended
on a bad note

in order not to separate i edited the parts
of us i didn't want to see the sight of -
the errors burn my pupils, misspellings and
misreading feeling ~~crossed out~~ and being
counted out. cross-references to past
indiscretions, you are my unlearned lesson

constant progression gets you past what
we couldn't compound and you get a
rebound even with infidelity, i still love you
incredibly (control my emotions) you can't
have the best of me

words build hope. can't even exchange
sentences, the space is declarative, and
the disappointment is a run on together
but complete fragments apart

i thought i was smart but our grammar is
all fucked up. i needed u to conjoin our
statements but she is the comma that
keeps us apart - i refuse to accept your
friendship as a conciliation

you were the only prize now it's you i
gotta despise. the conditions of this
syntax gave me the inability to relax
trying to remove the grammatical errors
i relapse

Homies Shouldn't Be Lovers

The last time I saw him, I said, "Get out of here before I steal you from your girlfriend." At that moment I wondered if I have truly grown past the lovers of my past.

Have I been trying to cut soul ties with a pair of dull scissors?

Has this knowledge of-self sharpened my blade or am I the same?

If I don't fall for anything else, I will fall for familiarity. My prerequisite for my lover to also be my homie is a double edge sword. It gives romantic leniency to lovers who should have just been friends, making it hard to cut ties after things fall apart.

I strategically destroy relationships and keep super glue on deck so that I can mend things with men I said I'd never see again.

The last time I claimed "this was the last time" was just a layover to another again. Reconnection is easy and we're just ordinary people lifting the pages of our closed books to open the attachment to what could have been if we communicated better and understood each other's love languages.

You know women are from Venus, Men are from Mars.

Is it intentional that you don't give me what I need? Once we supersede separation, I'll be ready to cast this attachment aside. It will seem like I'm leaving you all by your lonely, but it's me recoiling into my safe space of isolation until our next conversation.

You might as well stay where you are.

Stay there with the girl who has a bigger attention span whose interest are not trivial, because if I really am a lover who should have just been a friend, I wouldn't do you dirty again

Lover's Fist

Blistering bruises
Black and blue confusion
I miss my lover's fist
Pounding against my healing skin
Shaking the earth inside me
Twisted words putting a chokehold on my mind
I felt a comforting touch from another, but I
yearn to be burned - I like the abuse
In a place where I can't rehabilitate
I need a psychiatrist to help me facilitate
this desire to be harmed by what I idolize
He blackens my eyes with emotion

Blinded

I can't see what's in front of me
It's scarring my unblemished health
He's building up my mind's walls
Filling the halls
Love like cholesterol
I had to put regret on pause
Grab a soul to help my ailing

He's failing

Passionately grinding into me with the vaccine
It's filled with his virus
To prevent me from being infected
I must first acknowledge that which sickens
Mysterious diagnoses
What's the condition?
My doctor doesn't know

Nightmares from my dream man
He grabs my hand and reveals the track marks
I wake up to my bad habit

Signs of an addict realizing I haven't
been fixed makes me throw fits

Foul language fills my retorts
Anxiety keeps me restless
My nights sleepless
My new man is in mourning
He would love to revive what's dead in me
It won't awaken
I can't stop wanting to be punished
I need affection in the form of physical abuse

Pulled, tugged, pushed, and shoved into the corner
by the one who hurts me deeply
Content with the brutality of my reality
I cover the pain with Chanel shades and laughter
Wondering if there's a happily ever after for girls
addicted to their lover's fist

Damnation

If my mental state was a city
then I'm in the concrete jungle
somewhere between Hell's Kitchen and Harlem
You're stuck in my intellectual traffic
Don't be manic, pick a side
Veer to the left cause you know you ain't right
We're about to even shit up tonight
Most times you have to ask
Usually, I get requested
I'm reality
You're perception
Whatever I do rolls off me
and looks good on you
Second hand...
Smoke will kill you too
Usually faster than inhaling will do
This is vengeance
and its omnipresent
You can't outrun me
cause I'm everywhere
So where do you think you're going?
You're cornered
Your back's against the wall
Your face closing in on my gun
My steel is hard
Open your mouth

Don't waste breath with apologies
Just pleasure my weapon
I'll be extracting all vital organs
fuck what your license says
Fill your stomach with excess air to make
room for the actions it couldn't handle
Get my nine, pull the trigger,
a bullet hits the surface of your heart
mid-beat
Consider this 808 and heartbreak
Help you maintain brain function
so, a mutual understanding of my insanity
can be agreed upon
Have I lost my mind?
Hell yes
Have you run out of time?
Hell yes!!
If hindsight is 20/20
and everything is everything,
how will you ever be able to view yourself
spread across the continents so that you
can never recover the contents
Looking for you is going to be like
a voyage to Atlantis

Impossible since it no longer exist
GPS can't find your flow
There's nowhere else to go
Burn your conscience top brimstone to
remove ill content
Eternal flames will keep your demons from
haunting my thoughts

Killing you to revive free-thinking
This is an intellectual revival
Let the church say amen
and pray over the excess bloodshed

Where's ya head?
I decapitated that
You're probably gonna have a hard time
finding that and if justice is in fact
blindfolded with an uneven scale

I just sent you to hell

Mirage

Some kind of fool I must have been to fall in love with a mirage
I know it's not real, a vision of everything I ever wanted to see

Everything I prayed for I thought I wouldn't get. I thought I was asking for too much.

God answered my prayer with conditions, you cannot stay

A fool I must have been to fall in love with a mirage.
I know you're not real. Every time I try to back away you pull me back, magnetic field. You're all I feel. The first time we kissed, you kissed me so hard I thought I would cry. It felt real. I wondered how this sight could escape me. Wrapped you around my hopes and wishes. This is the place faith misses.

A fool I must have been to fall in love with a mirage.

Like a fairytale and fable introducing themselves to a nightmare because the shoe fits and your kiss awoke me from danger's spell. Your dichotomy is between fantasy and never existing. I need Pinocchio to be a real boy and more than just a toy.

Some kind of fool I must have been to fall in love with a mirage.
I know you're not real. I often forget how the fibers that make up our love are synthetic. Pathetic to want a vision. Like trying to own a dream, your presence is deferred until you can be held on to like a reality

Some kind of fool I must have been to fall in love with a mirage
when I know ..... you're leaving

Things Remembered

Things remembered are more than token pieces of engraved sterling silver. They're pictures tucked in the back of your junk drawer where he looks handsome, and you look happy. Pictures you never throw away, you just shove them to the back because that "miss" just might get real. Real enough to revisit a stolen moment because sometimes you feel like you miss it, but you remember it wasn't real.

He was a flesh and blood figment of your imagination. Aspects of his character were merely fictional. Even if you saw him, the presence of what you loved wouldn't be there. A shell of a person would stand before you, void of your friend.

Things remembered:

The scent of your favorite flower
The taste of your favorite dessert
The sound of your laughter

Sometimes you will think that you miss it, then you'll remember that it wasn't real. Like tarnished costume jewelry, he lost his luster and shine, dull and your eyes can't pretend that they don't see it. You can't 'unknow' this shortcoming, this devastatingly tragic character trait.

He was better in your head, had more going for him in the illusions.

In broad daylight, you can see the flaws in his diamond, and you can't rock with him when curiosity tries to get the best of you.

Who wants to hear the untold story of your missing heart? It's the missing part that crosses your mind because not a day goes by

How it steals fragments of your joy?
How you really ain't loved nobody like that since?

It's almost comforting to secretly hold this torch for the things remembered and never forgotten. On the outside, it's wrapped in the prettiest package of strength and dignity, but in reality, a reminisce could be the demise of memories you've been hiding.

One well-spoken declarative sentence could bring tears to your eyes. How you can't outgrow not measuring up in his eyes. How it used to be you and you know you saw it and he felt it too, but it wasn't real, it just felt like it.

How could a lie be the realest thing that you've ever known?

Why would an angel say what the devil wants to know? How did the time slip away and you forget to stop loving what you can't have? How did your heart become the penny with the hole in it?

And you - You've prayed on it, read a few books, worked on finding yourself, cleaned the crevasses of your mind with steel wool, and still it's there...

in the back of your junk drawer
at the bottom of your treasure chest
In the subconscious of your mind when you're lying-in bed
next to the men who never measure up

It's almost as if you should have never had it so good because it's made you bad, and spoiled it for all the rest

It's like a confession that you can't get off your chest
It's such a beautiful sentiment but it's shameful when you notice it for yourself

That love is stronger than pride
Things remembered that you try to hide

That all this time has passed, and you still love the love that won't love you back

Disturbia

My privates throb in your direction
This is grotesquely sublime like an erection
My thoughts stand at attention
Your voice was like a command
I wish you would be quite
The noise erupts from your lips repeatedly
I am distracted again
Favorite purple ink pen
Stuck on Nirvana's plain
If it's true, that I love myself better than you
Then it's inconvenient the way my mind finds
you

My soul seems sacrificial like the movie about
the place between dusk and dawn
Trying to see beyond the surroundings
Even the quickest route home seems scenic
I've seen it

The math has one common denominator: location
The straight paved road may seem the easiest
My unique gravel will unravel
A reward more fulfilling than any simplicity can
provide
Stay quiet little bird
Easier to hide behind fluted stemware
Elixirs made for after-dinner delicacies
I remember you being slightly negligent
We'll work through it
That makes the previous thoughts irrelevant

There is no after
New acquaintances taste drunken nectar
from my lips
They become oblivious
Unaware that they are blank canvases
I paint your image
Spray your cologne and hope he doesn't notice
I still have you on
Realize his touch is not yours
Awakening is excruciating
You're nine inches deep in another woman
and still thinking about me
Casual exchanges hide more than meets the
eye
Handshakes cry
She seems contrived
She can't possibly have conversation like I
Boredom seeps through your pores
Unused notebook on the coffee table
I'm still attracted
You're a bad habit
I suppose you'll die hard
Like the sublime erection that you are
It's unhealthy to be around you
As I sit behind you
I know you're gone but your t-shirt is in my
top drawer
I fear corners at the thought you might be
around one
Demand thoughts to stop going 360 for you
If your goal was to drive me crazy
We've reached our destination

A Lie That You Choose to Believe

What looks like good communication today can be 'everything was a lie' tomorrow. What once looked and felt like love in today's light turns out to be clear manipulation and not just because of the woman on the other side of town. Not just because of the nights you didn't spend with me, but more so, because when you lie to me, you think I believe you.

Your false narrative isn't for me
This story is for you

Facing your truth would be unbearable. It would crack the foundation of the character you've developed and you're not ready to stop playing this role. Wouldn't it be easier to embrace the scoundrel that you are? He probably needs a hug. What felt endearing last year, I have acknowledged is abuse today.

You must have thought that I was a moron standing next to a gas pump at Exxon for inhaling every gaslit side comment, but I wanted to be seen as wonderful in your eyes.

I wanted to be that girl.
I wanted to be the envy of strangers when they realized that you were my possession.

My obsession was at times vain but my love for you was true, so I allowed you to mold me into the image you saw fit. I just wasn't prepared to be written out of the script.

I thought that I had given a masterful performance of a woman that you could love, but the casting director in your mind saw another girl. One from the other side of town. A girl with wider hips and looser lips. A girl who wouldn't catch on to the man behind the curtain.

What's unresolved today will remain unresolved tomorrow if you never address it, and I dressed you in garments that you could never fit. Deep conversations, understanding, friendship

Those aren't labels you can afford; you'd rather wear knockoffs. A dollar saved is a dollar spent, depending on your intent. You'd rather spend your time spinning a web of lies around the hearts that cry after you zip up your pants. After you're gone it will almost be like you were never here. Just scars of disrepair that you told me were tattoos. You'll pump yourself up with the belief that you could have me again if you really wanted to, but that's just a lie that you choose to believe when you lay with the woman on the other side of town

About the Author

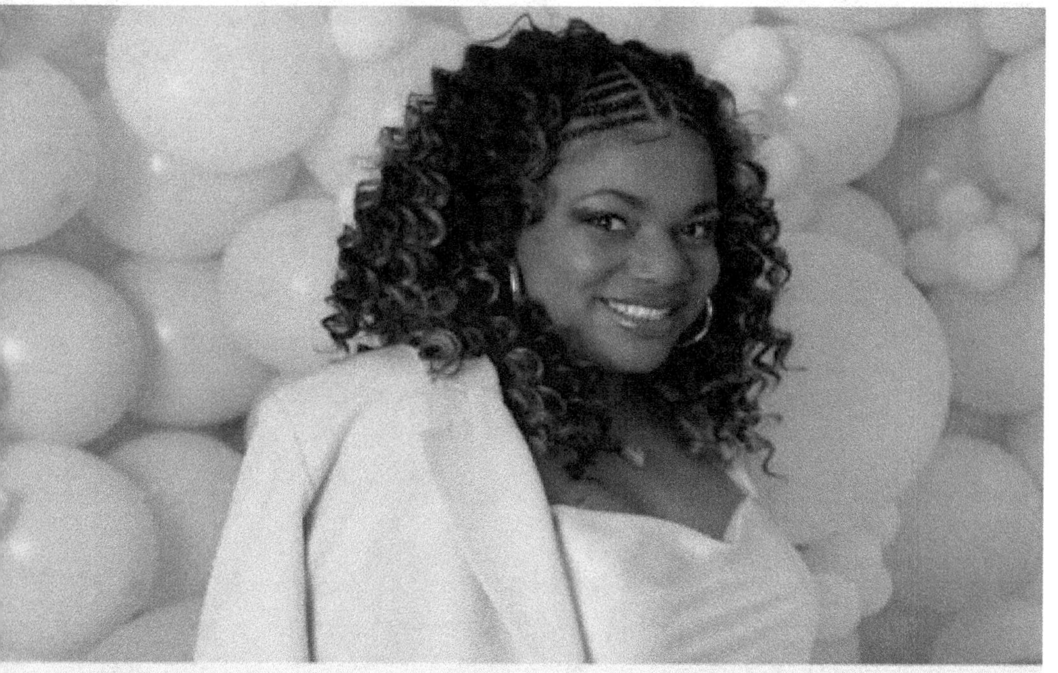

Laura Wize is a writer, podcast host, and content creator. Often referred to as Oh Wize One, Laura is outspoken and passionately believes in the transformative power of living life on her own terms. You can find her drinking mimosas at brunch or shopping in her hometown of Cincinnati, Ohio.

@ohwizeone

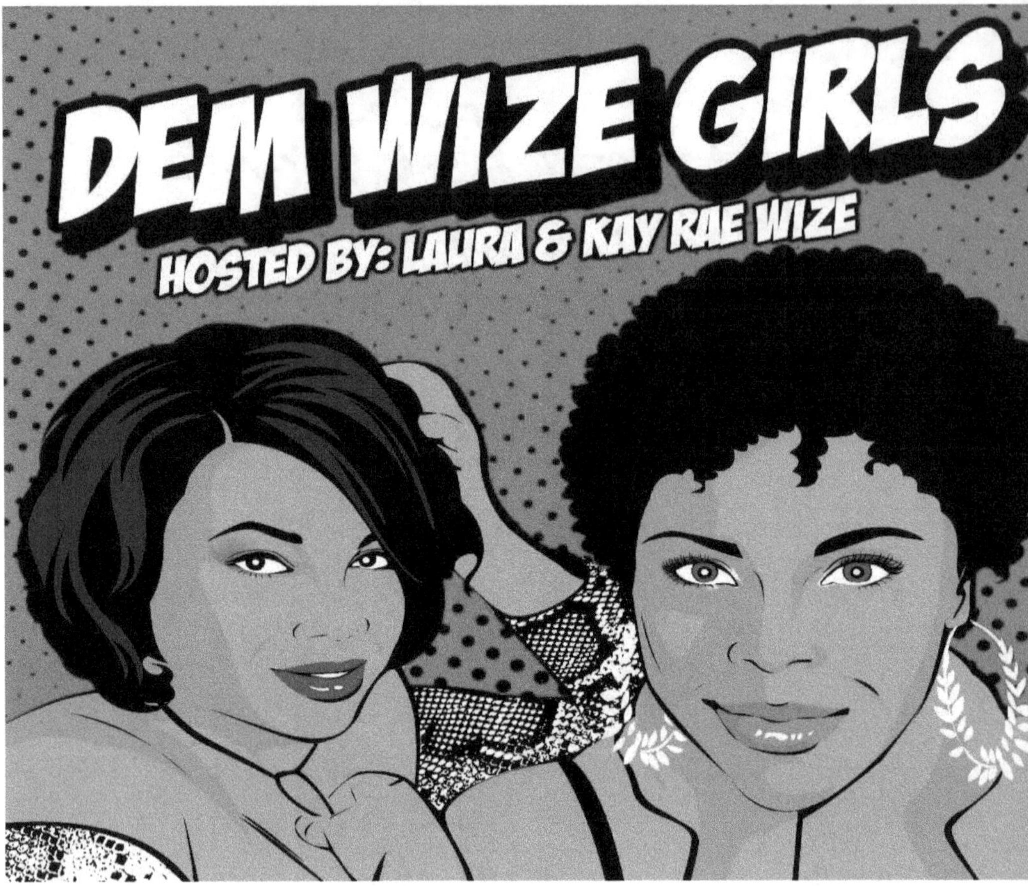

DEM WIZE GIRLS

HOSTED BY: LAURA & KAY RAE WIZE

Wize is their name, and wise is their game. Laura and Kay Rae Wize are two 30 somethin' sister-sistas who are glad 30 is not the new 20 because they embrace the wizdom that comes with age.

As Black women, we just want to BE our authentic selves, think as individuals to form opinions, and have a sense of self before societal expectations are thrusted upon us. The girl in us has questions but the woman in us needs answers.

Be Honest
and
Leave a Review

amazon goodreads

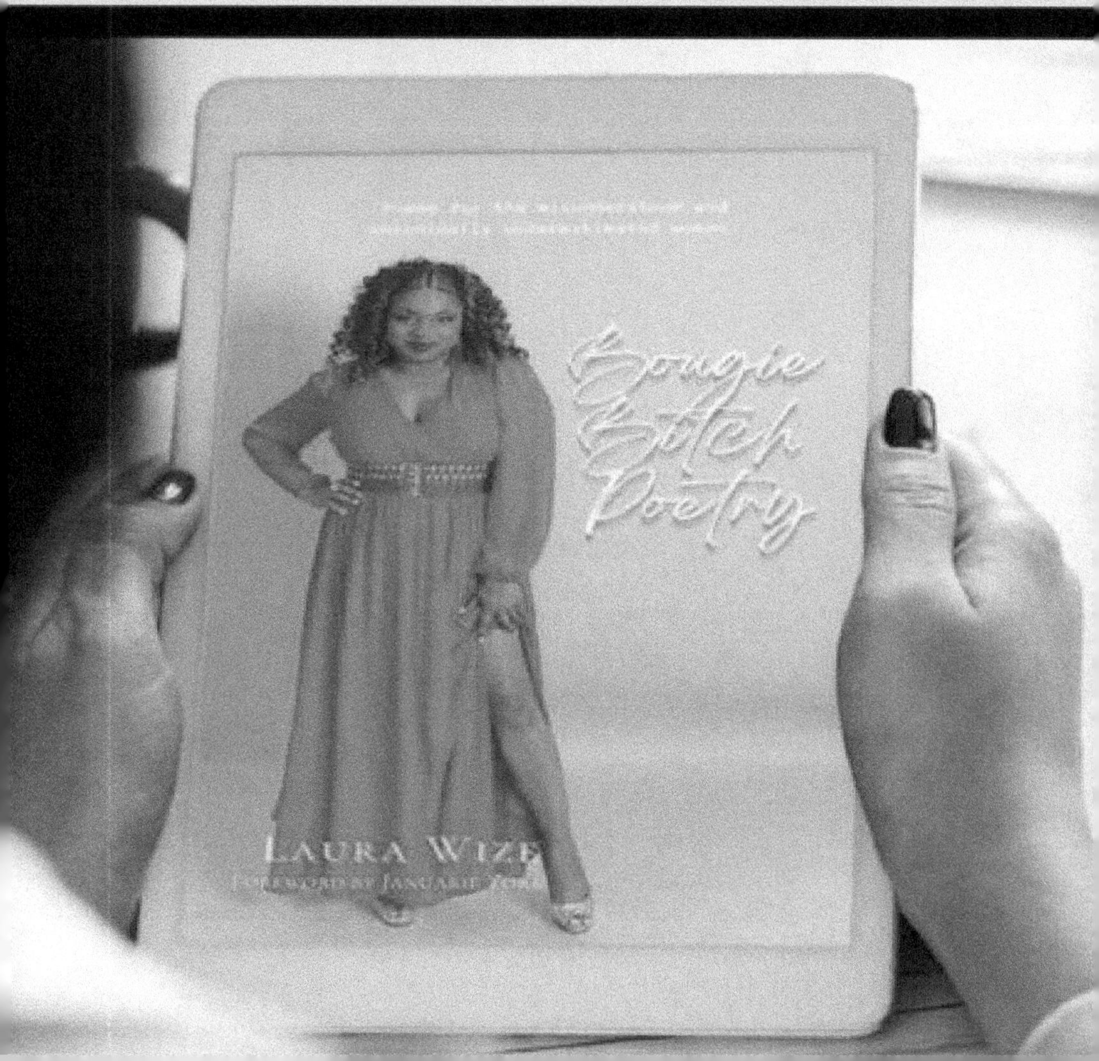

www.ingramcontent.com/pod-product-compliance
Lightning Source LLC
LaVergne TN
LVHW010627100826
845148LV00014B/3152

* 9 7 9 8 9 8 5 1 9 8 7 5 1 *

COMMUNION